W9-BKL-136

Vehicle-Mania!

Aero-Mania!

By Bill Gunston

Gareth Stevens Publishing
A WORLD ALMANAC EDUCATION GROUP COMPANY

Please visit our web site at: www.garethstevens.com
For a free color catalog describing Gareth Stevens Publishing's list
of high-quality books and multimedia programs, call 1-800-542-2595 (USA)
or 1-800-387-3178 (Canada). Gareth Stevens Publishing's fax: (414) 332-3567.

Library of Congress Cataloging-in-Publication Data

Gunston, Bill.
    Aero-mania! / by Bill Gunston. — North American ed.
        p. cm. — (Vehicle-mania!)
    Includes index.
    Contents: Airbus A380 — SR-71 Blackbird — Boeing 747 — B-2 Spirit — B-52 Stratofortress—
Concorde — Eurofighter Typhoon — F-117A Nighthawk — Harrier — F-35 Joint Strike Fighter —
Space Shuttle — Voyager — X-43A.
    ISBN 0-8368-3780-0 (lib. bdg.)
    1. Airplanes—Juvenile literature. [1. Airplanes. 2. Airplanes, Military.] I. Title. II. Series.
TL547.G8897 2003
629.133'34—dc21   2003042800

This North American edition first published in 2004 by
Gareth Stevens Publishing
A World Almanac Education Group Company
330 West Olive Street, Suite 100
Milwaukee, Wisconsin 53212

This U.S. edition copyright © 2004 by Gareth Stevens Inc. Original edition copyright © 2003 ticktock Entertainment Ltd.
First published in Great Britain in 2003 by ticktock Media Ltd., Unit 2, Orchard Business Centre, North Farm Road,
Tunbridge Wells, Kent, TN2 3XF, United Kingdom.

We would like to thank: Sam Petter, Keith Faulkner of Jane's Defence Weekly, and Elizabeth Wiggans.

Gareth Stevens Editor: Jim Mezzanotte
Gareth Stevens Art Direction: Tammy Gruenewald

Photo credits: Corbis: 4-5, 9b, 26-27; Aviation Picture Library: 6-7, 8-9c, 10-11, 16-17, 18-19, 20-21, 30-31; Lockheed: 22-23;
NASA: 12-13, 24-25, 28-29; Skyscan: 14-15.

Printed in Hong Kong

1 2 3 4 5 6 7 8 9 07 06 05 04 03

CONTENTS

AIRBUS A380

Did You Know?

The A380-800F is an A380 that will carry **cargo** instead of passengers. It will carry up to 162 tons (147 metric tons) of cargo.

Ever since the first plane took to the skies, designers have worked on creating bigger aircraft. In 1957, the American company Boeing began making the large 707. Then, in 1970, it produced the even larger 747. In 2006, a new giant will begin flying — the A380. It will be built by Airbus, a group of European companies.

The A380 has two engines on each wing. These engines produce a tremendous amount of **thrust**.

The **fuselage** of the A380 is deeper and wider than the fuselage of a 747.

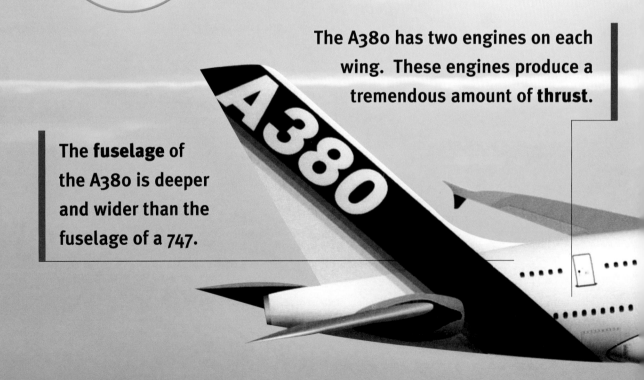

The standard A380 will have room for 854 passengers, and a longer version will seat 1,000 people. The plane will have a play area for children, and it will even have a shopping mall!

FACTS AND STATS

First Year: 2006

Origin: Europe

Length: 240 feet (73 meters)

Wingspan:
261.8 feet (79.8 m)

Maximum Weight:
650 tons (590 m tons)

Number of Crew: 2

Load: Up to 1,000 passengers or 162 tons (147 m tons) of cargo

Engines:
4 Rolls-Royce engines, each rated at 79,997 pounds (36,280 kilograms) of thrust, or 4 Engine Alliance engines, each rated at 81,592 pounds (37,003 kg) of thrust

Maximum Speed: 588 miles (946 kilometers) per hour

Range: 9,378 miles (15,089 km)

SR-71 BLACKBIRD

In 1960, a U.S. spy plane flying over Russia was shot down. Designers then created a plane that flew so fast and high it could not be shot down — the SR-71 Blackbird. First built in 1962, this spy plane is packed with cameras and other special **surveillance equipment**. After years of dangerous missions, no Blackbird has ever been lost.

Did You Know?

A Blackbird once flew from New York to London in 1 hour and 55 minutes.

The Blackbird was a secret project. U.S. president Lyndon Johnson did not admit it existed until 1964.

Each **jet engine** creates enough thrust to power an ocean liner. The large spikes catch air to keep the plane balanced in flight.

The Blackbird is made of a special metal called **titanium alloy**. This metal can withstand the incredible heat that is produced from flying at very high speeds.

BOEING 747

On April 13, 1966, Boeing received its first order for a new plane it was going to build — the 747. This huge plane became known as the "jumbo jet." Today, Boeing 747s are used around the world to carry passengers and cargo.

Did You Know?

The **wingspan** of a 747 is longer than the distance of the first powered flight by the Wright brothers.

A 747 can carry up to 550 passengers. It is the first wide-body plane ever built and has two aisles in the passenger cabin.

Modern 747s do not look much different than earlier models, but their engines are much more powerful.

FACTS AND STATS

First Year: 1970

Origin: United States

Length:
Up to 232 feet (70.7 m)

Wingspan:
Up to 212.9 feet (64.9 m)

Maximum Weight:
460 tons (418 m tons)

Load: 550 passengers or 124 tons (113 m tons) of cargo

Number of Crew: 4

Engines: 4 Pratt & Whitney, Rolls-Royce, or General Electric engines, each rated at 57,010 pounds (25,855 kg) to 62,011 pounds (28,123 kg) of thrust

Maximum Speed:
561 miles (903 km) per hour

Range: 8,681 miles (13,968 km)

The 747-400F cargo model has a nose that opens for loading cargo containers. The containers can weigh up to 124 tons (113 m tons)

B-2 SPIRIT

The B-2 Spirit is one of the most advanced planes in the world. It is used by the U.S. Air Force as a bomber plane, and it was designed to be almost invisible to **radar** so it will not be shot down. The B-2 has an unusual appearance. Some people think the plane looks like it came from another planet!

Did You Know?

The surface of the B-2 is jet black in color and very smooth. All joints between parts are concealed.

The B-2 is really just a giant wing. The plane has bulges that hide its engines, weapons, and cockpit.

The **cockpit** of the B-2 has space for just two crew members. The rest of the cockpit is full of computer-controlled flight equipment.

FACTS AND STATS

First Year: 1989

Origin: United States

Length: 69 feet (21 m)

Wingspan:
171.9 feet (52.4 m)

Maximum Weight:
400,069 pounds (181,437 kg)

Number of Crew: 2

Load: Weapons

Engines:
4 General Electric
F118-GE-110 turbofan
engines, each rated at
19,003 pounds (8,618 kg)
of thrust

Maximum Speed:
630 miles (1,014 km)
per hour

Range:
7,644 miles (12,300 km)

The B-2 is full of sophisticated equipment that reduces heat and noise so the plane can fly undetected. It is the world's most expensive aircraft.

B-52 STRATOFORTRESS

After World War II, the U.S. Air Force asked designers at Boeing to create a new bomber that could fly long distances. They designed the B-52 Stratofortress, a huge jet bomber with eight engines. A B-52 was first flown in 1952. Since then, B-52s have been used in many combat missions.

Did You Know?

The B-52 has **ejection seats** so the crew can escape the plane in case of an emergency.

The B-52 has **sensors** that let pilots fly the plane very close to the ground during combat missions.

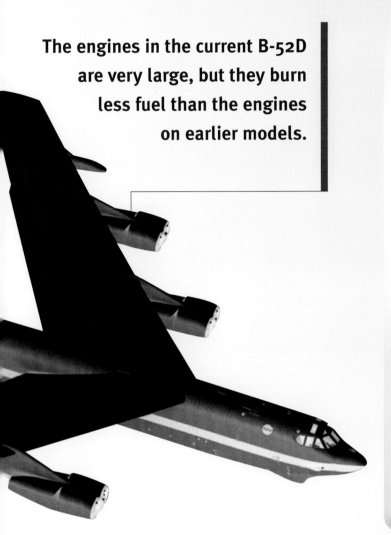

The engines in the current B-52D are very large, but they burn less fuel than the engines on earlier models.

FACTS AND STATS

First Year: 1952

Origin: United States

Length:
161 feet (49 m)

Wingspan:
185 feet (56.4 m)

Maximum Weight:
566,107 pounds
(256,738 kg)

Number of Crew: 6

Load: Weapons

Engines:
8 Pratt & Whitney TF33
turbofan engines, each
rated at 17,003 pounds
(7,711 kg) of thrust

Maximum Speed:
595 miles (957 km) per hour

Range:
12,566 miles (20,219 km)

A B-52 has a long **range,** and it can be refueled by another plane while flying. B-52s can fly almost anywhere in the world.

CONCORDE

In 1962, the governments of Britain and France began working together to create a **supersonic** plane called the Concorde. This amazing plane can cruise at **Mach** 2, which is twice the speed of sound. The Concorde can travel a long distance in a very short period of time. On the Concorde, a flight from London to New York lasts just over three hours.

Did You Know?

When the Concorde is in flight, it heats the air around it. This heat causes the plane to expand!

The Concorde's slim fuselage and triangular wings help it fly more than twice as fast as any other passenger plane.

The entire nose of the Concorde folds down so the pilot has better visibility during takeoff and landing.

FACTS AND STATS

First Year: 1977

Origin: Britain/France

Length:
204 feet (62.2 m)

Wing Span:
84 feet (25.6 m)

Maximum Weight:
204 tons (185 m tons)

Number of Crew: 2

Load: Up to 140 passengers

Engines:
4 Rolls-Royce/SNECMA
Olympus S93 turbojets,
each rated at 38,058 pounds
(17,260 kg) of thrust

Maximum Speed:
1,350 miles (2172 km)
per hour

Range:
4,509 miles (7,255 km)

With the huge thrust of four powerful engines, the Concorde can reach 225 miles (362 km) per hour in just 30 seconds after takeoff.

EUROFIGHTER TYPHOON

To build the Eurofighter Typhoon, the governments of Britain, Germany, Italy, and Spain all worked together. Creating a new plane can be very expensive, but these countries were able to share the cost of making the Typhoon. This powerful fighter plane is extremely fast.

Did You Know?

The idea for the Eurofighter dates back to 1979, but the first Eurofighter Typhoon was not built until more than twenty years later.

Only 15 percent of the outside of the Typhoon is made of metal. The rest is mainly lightweight **carbon fiber** that allows the plane to cruise at great speeds without overheating.

FACTS AND STATS

First Year: 2002

Origin: Europe

Length:
52.5 feet (16 m)

Wingspan:
36 feet (11 m)

Maximum Weight:
46,305 pounds (21,000 kg)

Number of Crew:
1 or 2

Load: Weapons

Engines:
2 Eurojet EJ200 turbofans,
each rated at 20,004 pounds
(9,072 kg) of thrust

Maximum Speed:
1,323 miles (2,129 km)
per hour

Range:
1,800 miles (2,896 km)

The Typhoon has a large triangular wing in back and small wings called foreplanes on each side of the nose. It comes in one- or two-seat versions.

With its powerful twin engines, the Typhoon can accelerate to Mach 1 — the speed of sound — in under 30 seconds. The Typhoon can also take off in just 5 seconds!

F-117A NIGHTHAWK

The F-117A Nighthawk is a special fighter plane used by the U.S. Air Force. The unusual shape of the F-117A helps it be almost invisible to radar. It can be refueled in midair, so it can travel almost anywhere in the world. First flown in 1981, the F-117A was created in complete secrecy. It is built by the American company Lockheed.

Did You Know?

The only parts of the F-117A that are not black are the windows.

The F-117A has hundreds of flat surfaces that cannot be detected by enemy radar.

The weapons for an F-117A are carried inside the plane. Special doors open and shut very quickly to release them.

FACTS AND STATS

First Year: 1981

Origin: United States

Length: 65.9 feet (20.1 m)

Wingspan:
43.3 feet (13.2 m)

Maximum Weight:
52,510 pounds (23,814 kg)

Number of Crew: 1

Load: Weapons

Engines:
2 General Electric F404-F1D2 turbofan engines, each rated at 10,802 pounds (4,899 kg) of thrust

Maximum Speed:
700 miles (1,126 km) per hour

Range:
1,500 miles (2,414 km)

Three F-117A Nighthawks are on display in the United States. An F-117A can be seen at the United States Air Force Museum in Ohio.

HARRIER

The Harrier is one of the most unusual planes in the world. This military plane is known as a Vertical Takeoff and Landing (VTOL) aircraft — it can take off and land vertically, like a helicopter. The first Harriers were built in Britain in the 1960s. Today, many countries use the Harrier, including Britain, the United States, Italy, Spain, and India.

Did You Know?

The U.S. Marine Corps has been using Harriers since the 1970s. The planes flew in combat missions during the Gulf War.

This single-seat Sea Harrier takes off and lands from ships. The Harrier also comes in two-seater and trainer versions.

Pilots in Harriers can perform complex movements to confuse pilots in enemy planes.

FACTS AND STATS

First Year: 1969

Origin: Britain

Length: 46.3 feet (14.1 m)

Wingspan: 43.3 feet (13.2 m)

Maximum Weight: 31,005 pounds (14,061 kg)

Number of Crew: 1 or 2

Load: Weapons

Engines: 1 Rolls-Royce Pegasus turbofan engine rated at 19,003 pounds (8,618 kg) of thrust

Maximum Speed: 700 miles (1,126 km) per hour

Range: 1,700 miles (2,735 km)

A Harrier's engine has two **nozzles.** They blast downward for takeoff and landing, to the rear for high speed, and forward to slow down.

F-35 JOINT STRIKE FIGHTER

The new F-35 Joint Strike Fighter (JSF) is actually three planes in one. The U.S. Air Force will use the F-35A, the U.S. Marine Corps will use the F-35B, and the U.S. Navy will use the F-35C. Production of the F-35 should begin in 2008.

Did You Know?

The British Royal Air Force and Navy plan to use the F-35B. It is a Short Takeoff and Vertical Landing (STOVL) plane, so it can land like a helicopter.

Over 80 percent of the parts in the F-35 are the same for each model.

Unlike other versions of the F-35, the F-35B will have a large fan behind the cockpit to provide vertical lifting power.

FACTS AND STATS

First Year: 2008

Origin: United States

Length: 50.5 feet (15.4 m)

Wingspan:
Up to 43.6 feet (13.3 m)

Maximum Weight:
60,009 pounds (27,215 kg)

Number of Crew: 1

Load: Weapons

Engines:
1 Pratt & Whitney
F135 engine rated at
40,008 pounds (18,144 kg)
of thrust and 1 Rolls-Royce
Allison engine-driven lift
fan (on X-35B only)

Maximum Speed:
1,058 miles (1,702 km)
per hour

Range:
1,380 miles (2,220 km)

The F-35C will be used on aircraft carriers. It has folding wings so it will take up less space on a ship, and it also has a hook that catches on the ship when it lands.

SPACE SHUTTLE

The first space flights used rockets with tiny capsules on top that floated back to Earth on **parachutes**. Then, in 1981, the National Aeronautics and Space Administration (NASA) launched the Space Shuttle. For the first time, a space vehicle returned to Earth by landing like an airplane.

Did You Know?

After takeoff, the **booster rockets** fall into the ocean. They are recovered and used again.

The front of the **orbiter** has room for ten people, and the central part can carry **satellites** and other cargo. Three large rocket engines are located in back.

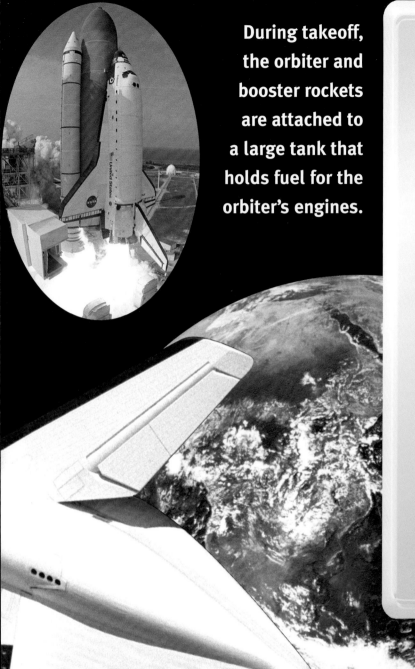

During takeoff, the orbiter and booster rockets are attached to a large tank that holds fuel for the orbiter's engines.

FACTS AND STATS

First Year: 1981

Origin: United States

Length: 184 feet (56.1 m)

Wingspan: 78 feet (23.8 m)

Maximum Weight:
2,249 tons (2,041 m tons)

Number of Crew: Up to 10

Load:
Satellites, parts for the International Space Station, and other cargo

Engines:
3 orbiter engines with a combined thrust of 595 tons (540 m tons) and 2 booster rockets with a combined thrust of 2,876 tons (2,610 m tons)

Maximum Speed:
17,440 miles (28,060 km) per hour

Range: 115 miles to 400 miles (185 km to 644 km)

After takeoff, the orbitor separates from the fuel tank and booster rockets. When the orbitor returns to Earth, it glides without engine power onto a runway and is slowed down by a large parachute.

VOYAGER

On December 23, 1986, a strange-looking plane called Voyager landed at Edwards Air Force Base in California. Voyager had taken off from the same runway nine days before, and when it landed, it became the first plane in history to fly non-stop around the world without refueling.

Voyager has an engine at either end of the central fuselage, and it has a total of seventeen fuel tanks. The two pilots who flew Voyager were in a very cramped space!

Most of Voyager was made of carbon fiber and paper. At rest, Voyager's flexible wings scraped the ground, but in flight they curved upward like the wings of a bird.

FACTS AND STATS

First Year: 1985

Origin: United States

Length:
29.2 feet (8.9 m)

Wingspan:
110.9 feet (33.8 m)

Maximum Weight:
9,698 pounds (4,398 kg)

Number of Crew: 2

Engines:
2 Teledyne Continental engines rated at 130 **horsepower** (hp) (front) and 110 hp (rear)

Maximum Speed:
122 miles (196 km) per hour

Range:
27,455 miles (44,175 km)

Voyager is one of many airplanes that Bert Rutan (right) created. Bert's brother, Dick Rutan, and a woman named Jeana Yeager flew Voyager around the world.

X-43A

Did You Know?

The X-15 was the first plane to fly at hypersonic speeds. First flown in 1959, it reached a speed of over 4,500 miles (7,240 km) per hour.

The amazing X-43A is an experimental plane. NASA will use it to learn more about flying at high speeds in the upper part of the **atmosphere**. It will fly at **hypersonic** speeds — over Mach 5, or more than five times the speed of sound. The **unmanned** X-43A is first dropped from a plane. Then, it flies high above Earth.

The X-43A is attached to the front of a rocket. After the rocket fires, it separates from the X-43A, and the plane's incredibly powerful **scramjet engine** takes over.

The X-43A will reach speeds between Mach 7 and Mach 10, or between 4,620 miles and 6,600 miles (7,434 km and 10,619 km) per hour. The plane will fly up to 19 miles (30 km) above the surface of Earth.

FACTS AND STATS

First Year: 2001

Origin: United States

Length:
12.1 feet (3.7 m)

Wingspan:
4.9 feet (1.5 m)

Maximum Weight:
2,800 pounds (1,270 kg)

Number of Crew:
Unmanned at present

Engine:
1 hydrogen-fueled scramjet engine

Maximum Speed:
6,600 miles (10,619 km) per hour

Range: Unknown

The first flight of an X-43A took place on June 2, 2001, when an X-43A attached to a Pegasus rocket was dropped from a B-52. During the flight, however, the plane broke up. NASA is still trying to figure out what went wrong.

GLOSSARY

atmosphere: the air that surrounds Earth.

booster rockets: on the Space Shuttle, rockets that provide extra power for taking off.

carbon fiber: a threadlike material that is light and very strong.

cargo: a shipment that a vehicle carries from one place to another.

cockpit: the part of a plane that holds the pilot and other crew members.

ejection seats: seats that pop out of an airplane so that crew members can escape by floating to the ground on parachutes.

fuselage: the central body of an airplane that holds the crew, passengers, and cargo.

horsepower: a unit of measurement for an engine's power that was originally based on the pulling strength of a horse.

hypersonic: more than five times the speed of sound.

jet engine: an engine that moves a plane forward by sending a powerful blast of gases out of its rear opening. Most military planes and large passenger planes use jet engines.

Mach: a measurement of speed based on the speed of sound, which is 700 miles (1,126 km) per hour. Mach 1 equals the speed of sound.

nozzles: on the Harrier, small openings that can let out powerful blasts of gases from the engine in several different directions.

orbiter: on the Space Shuttle, the vehicle that holds the crew and cargo and returns to Earth by landing like an airplane on a runway.

parachutes: devices with large, umbrella-like canopies that can slow down people or objects falling from the sky or vehicles rolling on the ground.

radar: a system that finds distant objects, such as airplanes, by using invisible radio waves.

range: the distance an airplane can fly without refueling.

satellites: machines that circle Earth in space and are used for many different jobs, such as providing information to scientists or sending television signals to different parts of the world.

scramjet engine: an experimental jet engine designed for planes that travel at extremely high speeds.

sensors: devices that can detect things for a pilot, such as weather conditions, other planes, or the ground.

supersonic: faster than the speed of sound.

surveillance equipment: devices used to spy on a person or place.

thrust: the pushing power of a jet engine or rocket, usually measured in pounds or kilograms.

titanium alloy: a light, strong metal that can withstand very high heat.

unmanned: having no people on board.

wingspan: the distance from the tip of one wing to the tip of the other wing on an airplane.

INDEX